Sharks

JUST WHEN YOU THOUGHT IT WAS SAFE TO OPEN A BOOK!

Use LOTS of stickers of sea creatures to fill this scene. But watch out!

Meet the family

Family comes first. Well, maybe food comes first. But family is important, too. The more than 400 kinds of shark in the world are all related. It's one big, hungry family!

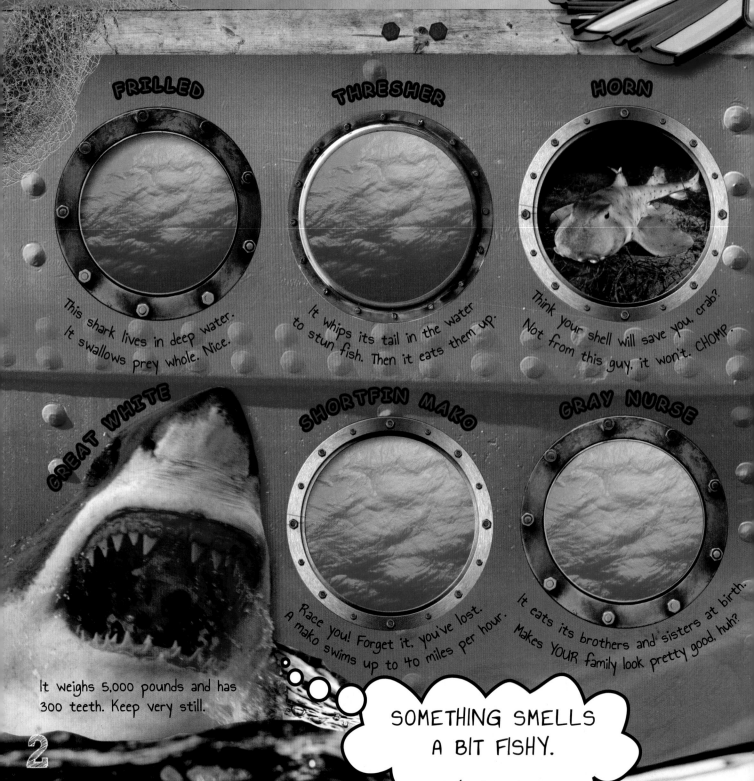

FRILLED

This shark lives in deep water. It swallows prey whole. Nice.

THRESHER

It whips its tail in the water to stun fish. Then it eats them up.

HORN

Think your shell will save you, crab? Not from this guy, it won't. CHOMP.

GREAT WHITE

It weighs 5,000 pounds and has 300 teeth. Keep very still.

SHORTFIN MAKO

Race you! Forget it. You've lost. A mako swims up to 40 miles per hour.

GRAY NURSE

It eats its brothers and sisters at birth. Makes YOUR family look pretty good, huh?

SOMETHING SMELLS A BIT FISHY.

Most sharks don't like to eat people. There's not enough meat on our bones!

WHY DID THE SHARK CROSS THE CORAL REEF?

TO GET TO THE OTHER TIDE.

OCEANIC WHITETIP

Your ship sank? This shark had you for lunch.

BULL

This shark likes to swim in warm, shallow water. Just like we do . . . .

COOKIE-CUTTER

Sounds all cute and cozy, right? Nope—it bites out cookie-shaped chunks of flesh.

NURSE

This guy sucks prey like a vacuum, then crushes it like a trash compactor.

GOBLIN

This shark lurks in the ocean's depths. It's not the prettiest—look at that snout!

Giganotosaurus

Anchisaurus

Ancient

It's the time of the dinosaurs. Hungry sharks race through prehistoric waters, looking for their next meals. Squalicorax chomps into

Squalicorax was a 15-foot killing machine with nasty, sharp triangular teeth. It looked like a modern great white shark.

Add stickers of ancient sea creatures. Who escapes Squalicorax and who gets eaten?

SWIM THIS WAY TO SAFETY

watch out for hot vents—OUCH!

oceans

anything it finds in the water. Fish. Turtles. Clumsy dinosaurs that fell in. It even takes on the giant lizard Tylosaurus—although it doesn't always win. . . .

Shark ATTACK!

Remember, great white sharks do not want to eat you. You are too bony. You are too much work. Seals, on the other hand, are plump and tasty. Rule number one for avoiding shark attacks: DO NOT LOOK LIKE A SEAL!

Here's a nice fat seal, out for a swim. Tra-la-la.

Uh-oh! A great white! It's moving in fast—25 miles per hour!

A flying shark? No. That leap's called a breach. Good catch!

Result? One full, happy shark. It won't need to eat again for a few weeks.

IT'S BEHIND ME, ISN'T IT?

shark

penguin

ray

sea lion

dolphin

6

 # Shark bait? Not you!

1 Be smart. If you're told to stay out of the water, STAY OUT OF THE WATER.

 **2** No shiny jewelry. No bright colors. Wearing them is like yelling, "Over here!"

 **3** If a great white comes over anyway, get out of the water, fast. DON'T PANIC.

 **4** Hit the shark on the eyes, gills, and snout. You heard us. Use your fist, your foot, even a rock.

teeth shaped to slice and tear flesh

5 Made it out of the water? Anything hurt? Get to a doctor. NOW!

WRONG WAY!

tuna

turtle

Seriously GROSS

A great white shark can bite other animals in half. Even those with tough shells—like turtles.

A great white doesn't chew its food. It rips off chunks. Then it swallows them. WHOLE.

A great white often takes a big, juicy bite out of its prey. Then it lets it bleed to death. Then it eats it.

When a great white is sick, it thrusts its stomach out of its mouth, then pulls it back in.

Record biters

Some sharks are extreme. Extremely awesome! ☺ But the most extreme record about sharks is the number of sharks that people kill every year. ☹ ☹ ☹ ☹ ☹

MY COUSIN ATE ONE OF THESE. NOT GOOD.

SMALLEST

RAREST

OLDEST LIVING

MOST COMMON

The frilled shark has lurked around for 95 million years. It has 300 teeth, with 3 hooks on each tooth. It eats prey half its size.

Shhh. The megamouth shark doesn't shout about where it's hiding. Only about 55 have ever been spotted.

Spiny dogfish are almost as common as pet dogs. But they're spinier. And not as good at fetching.

Dwarf lanternsharks are only about 7 inches long. But you can't miss them— they glow in the dark!

STICKERS
FOR PAGES
4-5

shark

penguin

ray

turtle

sea lion

dolphin

tuna

shark attack 1

shark attack 2

shark attack 3

shark attack 4

STICKERS
FOR PAGES
6-7

Megalodon
tooth

frilled

megamouth

shortfin mako

spiny dogfish

great
white

STICKERS
FOR PAGES
8–9

STICKERS
FOR PAGES
10–11

starfish

krill

anchovies

octopus

sea snail

fish

big fish

sardines

mullet

herring

sea lion

other shark

squid

sea urchin

STICKERS
FOR PAGES
12–13

dolphin

small fish

STICKERS
FOR PAGES
14–15

BIGGEST KILLERS?
Sharks kill fewer than 10 people a year. People kill about 100 million sharks a year. So who's the biggest killer? You're more likely to be killed by a hair dryer than by a shark.

WHAT DO YOU GET FROM A SHARK?

BIGGEST EVER
Megalodon lived 17–2 million years ago. It was up to 60 feet long and had 7-inch teeth. It even ate whales. Largest shark ever!

BIGGEST LIVING

TOOTHIEST

AS FAR AWAY AS POSSIBLE!

world's largest living fish

FASTEST

Want to grow   big and strong? Try   on, the tiny   als in water.   whale sharks! up to 59 feet long.

Whooosh. What was that? Oh, just a shortfin mako shark, speeding past at 40 miles per hour. It's the fastest shark in the ocean.

A person has 32 teeth. A great white shark has 300 teeth that grow in rows. As it loses one, another row moves forward. Smile!

9

Feeding frenzy

Are you an animal? Do you live in the sea? If you answered yes to both these questions, there's probably a shark somewhere that would LOVE to eat you.

seawater

plankton

tiny floating sea creatures

small fish

whale shark

Filter feeders, like whale sharks, sift MILLIONS of gallons of water to get a few pounds of food. They eat miniature creatures, such as tiny krill and itty-bitty plankton.

starfish

slimy

sea urchin

fish

fishy

nurse shark

squid

octopus

crunchy, with a creamy center!

sea snail

Bottom-feeders, like nurse sharks, eat creatures lurking on or near the seabed. These sharks live life in the slow lane. Favorite hobbies? Resting, dozing, and grabbing treats.

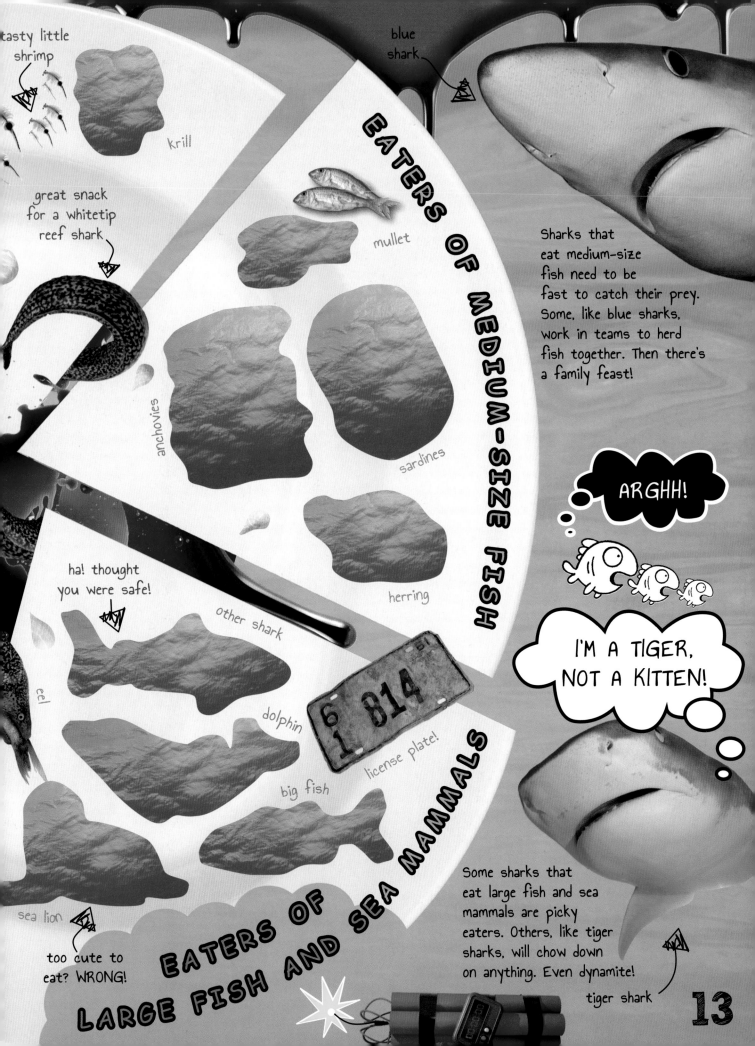

tasty little shrimp

krill

great snack for a whitetip reef shark

blue shark

mullet

EATERS OF MEDIUM-SIZE FISH

Sharks that eat medium-size fish need to be fast to catch their prey. Some, like blue sharks, work in teams to herd fish together. Then there's a family feast!

anchovies

sardines

herring

ha! thought you were safe!

other shark

eel

dolphin

6 1 814

license plate!

big fish

ARGHH!

I'M A TIGER, NOT A KITTEN!

sea lion

too cute to eat? WRONG!

EATERS OF LARGE FISH AND SEA MAMMALS

Some sharks that eat large fish and sea mammals are picky eaters. Others, like tiger sharks, will chow down on anything. Even dynamite!

tiger shark

13

Hand-build a hammerhead

Use stickers to make your very own shark.

great hammerhead

HEADS UP! Choose a crazy head. A hammerhead's head is filled with sensors that detect electricity in prey.

BODY TYPE Pick a sleek, streamlined body—good for gliding through the water efficiently.

EYE, EYE! Stick an eye on each end of your shark's "hammer." Now it can see up and down at the same time!

More sharks . . .

hammerhead   leopard   wobbegong   thresher

Produce a predator

great white

FINS OF FEAR
Help your shark balance and steer. Give it lots of fins. Most sharks have eight.

Hammerheads not scary enough for you? Now make something REALLY terrifying!

TEETH
Choose teeth that slice like razors. Or pierce like daggers. Or crush like mallets.

NOSE
Add a nose to seek out prey—especially if the prey is bleeding!

HELLO! MY NAME IS

STRONG TAIL
This helps speed after prey. Swim, little victims! Swim!

mako

nurse

bull

reef

great white

WHAT DO YOU CALL A FISH WITH NO EYES?

A FSH!

Image credits